# HISTORY HUNTERS

# DINOSAUR
# DIG

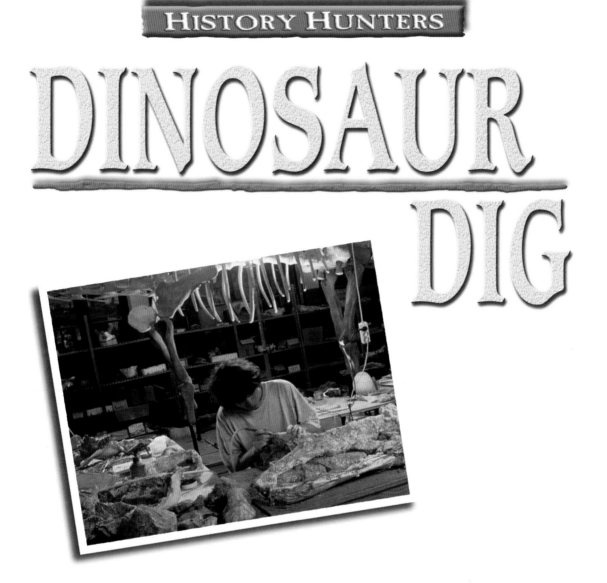

## by Dougal Dixon

**Gareth Stevens Publishing**
A WORLD ALMANAC EDUCATION GROUP COMPANY

**Please visit our web site at: www.garethstevens.com**
**For a free color catalog describing Gareth Stevens Publishing's**
list of high-quality books and multimedia programs,
call 1-800-542-2595 (USA) or 1-800-387-3178 (Canada).
Gareth Stevens Publishing's Fax: (414) 332-3567.

**Library of Congress Cataloging-in-Publication Data**

Dixon, Dougal.
  Dinosaur dig / by Dougal Dixon. — North American ed.
    p. cm. — (History hunters)
  Includes bibliographical references and index.
  Summary: Describes a research expedition to Montana to uncover and investigate a dinosaur skeleton.
  ISBN 0-8368-3739-8 (lib. bdg.)
  1. Dinosaurs—Juvenile literature. [1. Dinosaurs. 2. Archaeology.] I. Title. II. Series.
  QE861.5.D586  2003
  567.9—dc21                                                    2003045739

This North American edition first published in 2004 by
**Gareth Stevens Publishing**
A World Almanac Education Group Company
330 West Olive Street, Suite 100
Milwaukee, WI 53212 USA

This U.S. edition copyright © 2004 by Gareth Stevens, Inc. Original edition copyright © 2003 ticktock
Entertainment Ltd. First published in Great Britain in 2003 by ticktock Media Ltd., Unit 2, Orchard Business
Centre, North Farm Road, Tunbridge Wells, Kent, TN2 3XF. Additional end matter copyright © 2004 by
Gareth Stevens, Inc.

We would like to thank: Dr. Angela C. Milner at The Natural History Museum and Elizabeth Wiggans.

Illustrations by Luis Rey, John Alston, Simon Mendez and Dougal Dixon.

Gareth Stevens editor: Carol Ryback
Gareth Stevens cover design: Katherine A. Goedheer

Photo credits:
t=top, b=bottom, c=center, l=left, r=right, OFC=outside front cover, OBC=outside back cover
Airsport: 9tr. Alamy images: 3bl, 3br, 11cr, 13cr, 14tr. John Alston: 4bc, 5cr. Corbis: OFCbr, 8br,
10-11, 10tr, 12b, 15tr, 18-19, 20bl, 26-27, 28-29. Dougal Dixon: 4c, 10b, 16br. Everett Collection:
4br. Geoscience: 18bl, 18br. Masterfile: 8-9. Natural History Museum: 5t, 15bl. Simon Mendez: 5cr,
7tl, 7cl. Luis Rey: 5bl, 7cr, 23br, 24-25. Science Photo Library: 20-21t, 22tr.

Every effort has been made to trace the copyright holders, and we apologize in advance for any
unintentional omissions. We would be pleased to insert the appropriate acknowledgments in any
subsequent edition of this publication.

Printed in Hong Kong

1 2 3 4 5 6 7 8 9 07 06 05 04 03

Would you like to join an exciting dinosaur-digging expedition?

The characters accompanying you – Charlie Smith, Dr. Marilyn Petronella, and Professor Dean (Dino) Rockwell – are fictitious, but the facts about museums, paleontologists, and scientists represent an accurate view of their work. The dinosaur you are about to discover – <u>Phobosaurus charlii</u> – is also fictitious, but the characteristics and details of its life are based on facts about the family of dinosaurs known as tyrannosaurids.

Can't wait to learn more? Ready to dig for ancient clues?

Then welcome to the City Museum...

## CONTENTS

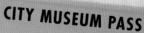

**CITY MUSEUM PASS**

**Name:** Dr. Marilyn Petronella
**Position:** Curator
**Department:** Paleontology

**Interests:** Dinosaurs, mammoths, digging, and rock climbing.

**CITY MUSEUM PASS**

**Name:** Charlie Smith
**Position:** Temporary Research Assistant
**Department:** Paleontology

**Interests:** Dinosaurs, mammoths and skateboarding.

TEMPORARY

# A FANTASTIC FIND

## Day 1

I am spending summer vacation as an assistant researcher in the paleontology department of the City Museum. Paleontologists study past life by examining fossils. I was working in a dusty basement storeroom when I made a fantastic discovery – a fossilized dinosaur bone!

My boss, Dr. Marilyn Petronella, says the museum's catalog number lists my fossil as the left maxilla (the upper jawbone) of a dinosaur known as Tyrannosaurus rex. But Dr. Petronella doesn't think this fossil is from a T. rex, even though the bone is definitely from the tyrannosaurid family.

I didn't know that dinosaurs had families! Apparently it's the same as it is with cats. Lions, tigers, and cheetahs all are cats, but each is slightly different and has its own scientific name. Dr. Petronella thinks that this fossil belongs to a completely new kind of tyrannosaurid. And I found it!

I found a bunch of old photographs and field notes from a 1920s expedition to Montana packed with the maxilla.

CM-3500

### Skull of Tyrannosaurus rex

The maxilla fits here.

2.5 – 3 feet
(0.75 – 1 meter)

A Tyrannosaurus rex maxilla has about 16 teeth on one side. A new tooth grew in if one fell out!

Our maxilla specimen has fewer teeth. It cannot be from a T. rex.

A T. rex in action in Jurassic Park. One of my favorite movies ever!

CM-008M

Paleontologists compare newly discovered dinosaur fossils to known fossils to help in identification.

**Daspletosaurus torosus**
(frightful, fleshy lizard)
Length: 29.5 ft (9 m)
Possible ancestor of T. rex. Smaller, but with a heavy head. Larger teeth than T. rex, but fewer of them.

The teeth on our specimen are more widely spaced.

**Nanotyrannus lancensis**
(dwarf tyrant, from the Lance geological formation)
Length: 13 ft (4 m)
Pygmy of the group. Some scientists think it is just a baby Albertosaurus.

Our specimen is much larger than this.

**Alioramus remotus**
(different branch, remote)
Length: 20 ft (6 m)
This dinosaur had a long narrow skull with horns along the crest. Lived in Asia.

Our specimen was found in Montana.

## Tyrannosaurs
where does our specimen fit in?

**Albertosaurus sarcophagus**
(lizard from Alberta, eater of the dead)
Length: 29.5 ft (9 m)
This animal was smaller and lighter than T. rex and possibly a fast runner.

Teeth do not quite match. Our specimen has larger teeth.

**Tyrannosaurus rex**
(tyrant lizard king)
Length: 39 ft (12 m)
T. rex was, as far as we know, the largest meat-eating dinosaur that ever lived.

Using the maxilla as a guide, our specimen is about two-thirds the size of a T. rex.

# A TRIP TO MONTANA

## Day 2

Our maxilla fossil was found in the badlands of Montana – one of the best places in the world to find dinosaur skeletons. Tyrannosaurs lived during the late Cretaceous period (about 95 to 65 million years ago) when what is now Montana was a river plain next to an inland sea.

Over eons of geologic activity, sand and silt from the ever-changing river courses and marine water levels buried a variety of dinosaurs and other animals. Today this section of Montana is dry and windy, and the land is eroding so fast that fossils almost pop out of rocks in front of your eyes!

Dr. Petronella's friend, Professor Dean Rockwell, who is an expert on tyrannosaurs, will join our dinosaur expedition!

What to Bring:

Hiking boots, backpack, hat, water bottle, sunscreen, traveler's checks. Temperatures can climb above 100°F (38°C) in summer.

Professor Rockwell will meet us at the airport in Missoula, Montana.

Professor Dean (Dino) Rockwell and Rex, his dog.

Over time, tree resin and anything stuck inside it may fossilize into the mineral amber. This piece of amber contains a fossilized insect.

# Professor Dino Rockwell says "Welcome to our Museum..."

**The museum was founded specifically to study North American dinosaur remains from the late Cretaceous period.**

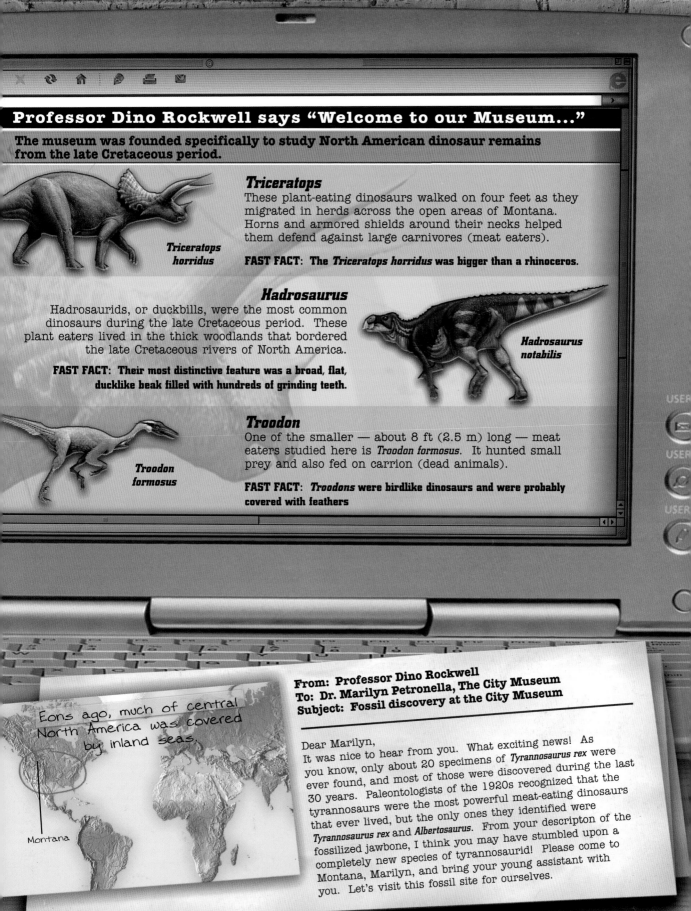

### Triceratops

These plant-eating dinosaurs walked on four feet as they migrated in herds across the open areas of Montana. Horns and armored shields around their necks helped them defend against large carnivores (meat eaters).

*Triceratops horridus*

**FAST FACT:** The *Triceratops horridus* was bigger than a rhinoceros.

### Hadrosaurus

Hadrosaurids, or duckbills, were the most common dinosaurs during the late Cretaceous period. These plant eaters lived in the thick woodlands that bordered the late Cretaceous rivers of North America.

*Hadrosaurus notabilis*

**FAST FACT:** Their most distinctive feature was a broad, flat, ducklike beak filled with hundreds of grinding teeth.

### Troodon

One of the smaller — about 8 ft (2.5 m) long — meat eaters studied here is *Troodon formosus*. It hunted small prey and also fed on carrion (dead animals).

*Troodon formosus*

**FAST FACT:** *Troodons* were birdlike dinosaurs and were probably covered with feathers

Eons ago, much of central North America was covered by inland seas.

Montana

From: Professor Dino Rockwell
To: Dr. Marilyn Petronella, The City Museum
Subject: Fossil discovery at the City Museum

Dear Marilyn,
It was nice to hear from you. What exciting news! As you know, only about 20 specimens of *Tyrannosaurus rex* were ever found, and most of those were discovered during the last 30 years. Paleontologists of the 1920s recognized that the tyrannosaurs were the most powerful meat-eating dinosaurs that ever lived, but the only ones they identified were *Tyrannosaurus rex* and *Albertosaurus*. From your descripton of the fossilized jawbone, I think you may have stumbled upon a completely new species of tyrannosaurid! Please come to Montana, Marilyn, and bring your young assistant with you. Let's visit this fossil site for ourselves.

# ABOVE THE BADLANDS

## Day 7

Finally! We are in Montana — or at least above it! I'm writing this from a hot-air balloon. Dino (Professor Rockwell said it was okay to call him that) brought us up here to show us the landscape. This is an awesome view!

Below us stretch Montana's prairies. Dino says that millions of dinosaur skeletons may lie under this flat surface. Over millions of years, layer upon layer of rock was deposited here by ancient rivers and oceans. Although most of the land looks as flat as a pancake, gullies and ravines crack and split the surface. Gullies — the huge, natural trenches worn in the rock by running water — and ravines — the narrow, v-shaped steep valleys — offer the best clues for where to start looking for fossils.

The pioneers nicknamed this uneven, rocky area the badlands because it was "bad land" — very difficult land to cross with their horses and covered wagons.

## THE FIRST TYRANNOSAURUS REX

**N**atural history enthusiasts will remember 1905 for many years to come. Barnum Brown, the great dinosaur hunter, has returned to Montana to dig up the skeleton of a new species of dinosaur he found in 1902. Brown is sending the skeleton to the American Museum of Natural History in New York. Henry Fairfield Osborn, paleontologist and director of the Museum, says that this is the largest meat-eating dinosaur ever discovered. It is named *Tyrannosaurus rex*, king of the terrible lizards.

In the late Cretaceous period, 75 million years ago, Montana's geography was very different from what we see today.

Rivers meandered across the plains, carrying sand and silt down from what are now the Rocky Mountains. These rivers deposited the sediments that formed the sand-stone rock of present-day Montana.

The ancestral Rocky Mountains are seen on the horizon.

Dinosaurs lived in the thick forests along the riverbanks.

The rivers flowed into a shallow inland sea that covered much of central North America. This ancient, inland sea stretched south to the Gulf of Mexico.

# LOCATING THE SITE

## Day 9

As I looked down on the prairie from the balloon, I wondered how we would ever pinpoint our dinosaur site. Dino says we must locate it visually by using landmarks seen in the old photographs. He says this method has worked before.

Dino's mobile home serves as our base camp. We drive to a different area every day, then explore on foot. Yesterday, I almost twisted my ankle scrambling down a scree slope. (Scree is the loose rubble that breaks off the cliffs and falls downslope.)

Then we saw a pinnacle just like the one in the photograph! It's unbelievable – not much has changed in the decades since the photograph was taken. Now we can mark the site with our global postioning system (gps) coordinates to find it again.

Paleontologist Scott Madsen exposes the lost dinosaur tracks.

## LOST FOOTPRINTS FOUND

**P**aleontologist Scott Madsen used old photographs to find dinosaur footprints that were believed lost forever in an Arizona desert. The fossil footsteps were first discovered in 1934 by paleoichnologist (someone who studies fossil footprints) Roland T. Bird. Although Bird photographed the trail of 200-million-year-old fossil footprints, he didn't record their location in any other way. More than half a century later, in 1986, Madsen decided to study the landscape features of Bird's photographs — which led him to the exact spot. He brushed away some sand to find the footprints.

The 1920s expedition notes say the fossilized jawbone was found in the rubble at the foot of this slope.

Fossils erode from rocks higher up on the slopes. We will start our search for more dinosaur remains up here.

Layers of sedimentary rock form the plains of Montana. Over millions of years, water gradually deposits layers of mud, sand, and other sediments that harden into rock. Scientists determine the age and geologic time period during which particular rock layers formed by measuring the age of each layer — or bed — of rock.

Sedimentary rock layers form from the bottom up in a process called "superposition." That means that younger rock layers overlie the older, deeper rock layers.

Climbers gear up to scale the cliff and look for more of the dinosaur.

**From: Charlie Smith**
**To: City Museum Paleontology Department**
**Subject: Exploring the Badlands**

Hi Everyone,
Montana is awesome! Professor Dino Rockwell drives us around as he describes the landscape and its dangers (like rattlesnakes!). Dino obtained permission from one of the local farmers for us to explore the area. We use a dirt road on the farmer's property to access the site. Dino also arranged for us to excavate the farmer's land if we find something.
Now that we have located the site using the old photograph, Dr. Petronella's hunch is that the rest of the skeleton may be closer to the top of the cliff. We will need climbing gear, such as ropes, climbing boots, and mountaineering picks, to reach the dig site. I will e-mail again tomorrow. I'm hopeful that I'll have good news about our search! — Charlie

USER 1

USER 2

USER 3

# THE SKELETON UNCOVERED

## Day 10

Dr. Petronella's hunch was right! When Dino rappelled down to the ledge, he found a string of fossil bones sticking out of the rock. He called them articulated cervical vertebrae, which means they are neck bones that are still joined together. Simply calling them neck bones is not precise enough, though. Scientists must use the correct anatomical terminology at all times so that anybody working on a skeleton knows exactly what part of the body the bones came from.

Dr. Petronella and I quickly scrambled down to help Dino scrape around in the loose sandstone. Just a few yards away in the same fossil bed, we found a disarticulated caudal vertebrae (a piece of tail bone). Disarticulated means it's not joined to the rest of the tail. With the neck and tail here, maybe we'll discover the whole skeleton buried in the rock!

Climbing around high rock faces is dangerous. Fossil hunters and excavators wear safety helmets to protect themselves. Goggles guard against eye injuries.

Searchers use basic tools like hammers and chisels during the exploratory phase of an expedition to check for additional bones buried deeper in the rock.

We found a string of articulated cervical vertebrae embedded in the rock.

Jimmy's flatbed truck is ready to haul.

**To: City Museum Paleontology Department from Charlie Smith
Subject: Planning an excavation**

Hi Everyone — Dr. Petronella thinks that the rest of the dinosaur's skeleton is buried in the cliff near its neck and tail! Dino says an official excavation could take as long as a year to organize. In addition to dozens of volunteer diggers, we will need some massive excavating equipment and a way to move our dinosaur — all for the lowest cost possible.

**From: Jimmy Pagelli of Jimmy's Trucking Service
Subject: Dinosaur bones moved — for free!**

Dear Dr. Rockwell — Congratulations on your recent dinosaur discovery! In exchange for advertising rights, I am offering your team the use of our front-end loader, as well as a flatbed truck to haul the fossil pieces to the museum. As you may recall, we offered you the same services for the *Triceratops* excavation last year. Best wishes for a successful dig — Jimmy Pagelli.

# STARTING WORK

## One year later

Wow! It's been a whole year since I searched for dinosaurs in Montana. Meanwhile, Dino and his team performed a small dig on the site. They found more bones and began a full-scale excavation. Workers removed hundreds of cubic yards of rock from above the specimen.

Over the winter, even more of the heavy work was completed. Jimmy's workers bulldozed a road right up to the excavation site, making it easy for trucks and four-wheel-drive vehicles to get up close to the buried fossil. It's just like a dinosaur drive-in!

Now the delicate work of excavating the skeleton begins. Dino recruited museum staff members, volunteers from all over the world, and ME to help.

Earthmovers clear a path to the site so that Jimmy's flatbed truck can remove the fossil.

For the first time in 75 million years, the dinosaur fossils will be exposed to air. They are very fragile and must be protected with a special varnish. We will "paint" the fossils with a varnish made from these white granules.

Fossil bones are extremely delicate. Dental instruments and fine brushes come in handy at this phase of the work.

We got on our hands and knees to chip away at the rock around the fossilized bones.

Jimmy's heavy equipment removed the overburden (the layer of rock on top of the fossil-bearing bed).

Pieces of wood that have turned to coal prove that our dinosaur lived near what was once a forest.

Deposits of sand and other sediments formed patterns in the ancient riverbed.

We found a petrified crocodile skull in a riverbed near the bottom of the cliff where our dinosaur is buried.

Laboratory techs will sort the fossilized insects and microscopic pollen grains from the samples of rocks and scree.

## The best day yet!

Now that the overburden is removed, we can see about 40 percent of the whole skeleton – a rare find. Most paleontologists are happy when they discover a single identifiable bone. We must record the positions of the bones before anything is moved. Bone positions provide many clues about how the animal lived and died.

Scientists often name a skeleton after the person who discovered it. They named our skeleton Marilyn, after Dr. Petronella. Other T. rex skeletons are named Stan, Sue, and Kathy. It would have been cool to call this one Charlie, but the paleontologists think it's a female!

This evening, in a pile of scree at the foot of the cliff, we found a huge section of skull. It looks as if it broke away from the ledge in one piece.

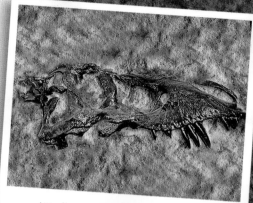

We found the right half of the skull. It looks as if the right maxilla matches our left maxilla specimen.

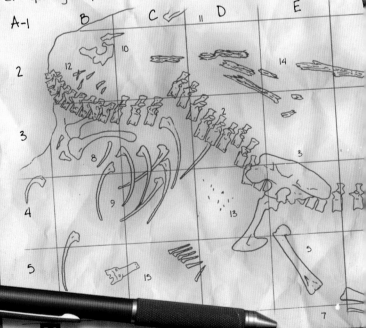

Researchers plot the locations of all fossils on a grid or "quarry map," before removing anything from the site.

Searchers plot the location of every fossil on a grid, so that scientists can study the positions of the bones at a later time. The way the bones lie hold many clues to how the dinosaur lived and died.

Performing a dinosaur dig is not easy. Experts and volunteers must work carefully and be very patient. If they dig too quickly or carelessly, it can damage a fossil.

G

## QUARRY MAP KEY

1. complete, articulated cervical vertebrae
2. complete, disarticulated dorsal vertebrae
3. Ninety percent complete pelvic girdle
4. caudal (tail) vertebrae – scattered
   – about 40 percent complete
5. right femur
6. right tibia
7. right fibula
8. shoulder girdle – complete
9. disarticulated rib cage
   – about 50 percent complete
10. scattered skull fragments
11. right humerus
12. scattered bone fragments
    – probably cervical ribs
13. field of broken teeth from
    a small theropod (meat eater)
    – possibly Troodon
14. coalified wood
15. crocodile skull

4

# A RACE AGAINST TIME

## The final day

We recorded all the information we need. It's time to prepare the skeleton for removal from the site for further study.

To prevent the fossils from crumbling or flaking away, we must cover them in plaster, just like doctors do when you break your leg. Dino says this technique was first used by a team of paleontologists back in 1876 – except they used rice pudding! (The story goes that the expedition's kitchen had plenty of rice pudding, but nobody liked it, so the scientists used the pudding to protect the fossils instead.)

Dino will cut the skeleton into sections, with big chunks of surrounding rock acting as splints. We will dig a trench around each section to free it from the site. We'll have to work fast. The rainy season is almost here and could wash part of the skeleton away.

We remove rock from beneath the fossil. Once it is free, we must protect the other side with the plaster wrap.

We'll cover the fossils with wet newspapers and then wrap them with burlap soaked in thick plaster.

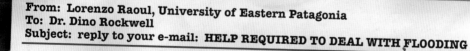

**From: Lorenzo Raoul, University of Eastern Patagonia**
**To: Dr. Dino Rockwell**
**Subject: reply to your e-mail: HELP REQUIRED TO DEAL WITH FLOODING**

Dino – Sorry to hear that you have run into bad weather. Here is what we did when a flood almost washed out our *Giganotosaurus* dig in Argentina last year: We cut a deep horseshoe-shaped trench in the hill around the entire specimen. The water flowed downhill into the trench and around our fossil. We also covered our find with plastic tarps that were tightly staked down to help keep the rain off the plaster castings. Hope this helps. Good luck!

**From: Charlie Smith**
**To: City Museum Paleontology Department**
**Subject: Marilyn stalks the badlands again!**

Success! We beat the storms and the floods. We got the dinosaur out before the roads washed away. Jimmy's heavy machinery and equipment reached the site with no problems. We reinforced the huge blocks of plaster with steel bars and loaded the skeleton piece by piece onto the flatbed truck. Once again, Marilyn is on the move across the badlands of Montana!

# IN THE LABORATORY

## Two weeks later

Marilyn is finally in the museum's laboratory. Specialized technicians called "preparators" will remove the matrix — the surrounding stone in which the fossils are embedded — from around Marilyn's bones. But before they begin, the preparators must know what steps were taken in the field to prepare the skeleton for shipping.

Dino and Dr. Petronella made a list of the glues and hardeners used on the fossils before they were wrapped in plaster. We also assigned a grid number and letter to each of the huge fossil blocks. After the preparators have finished preserving and preparing Marilyn's fossils for display, paleontologists and other scientists will travel here to study them in detail.

Dino says our timing was perfect. Erosion would have destroyed Marilyn within a few years if we hadn't discovered her.

## Watch our preparators as they prepare Marilyn for paleontological study and display.

View our laboratory as the team...

- unpacks Marilyn from her plaster casts.
- removes the matrix from around her bones.
- treats the fossil bones with preservative to toughen them.
- cleans oxidized material from the bones.
- repairs any bones that broke in transit.

Visit the new display featuring Marilyn's skeleton in the dinosaur gallery of the City Museum.

Once the project is completed, paleontologists from all over the world can study Marilyn's skeleton!

This tooth is almost ready for display. Teeth are made of enamel, a material harder than bone. Teeth preserve better than bone and need very little preparation.

Preparators use high-pressure air jets and tiny dental drills to clear rock and soft material from around the fossil.

# EXAMINING THE EVIDENCE

## Dinosaur detective!

Marilyn's skeleton is cleaned and prepared for study. Dr. Petronella says that in the old days paleontologists would just dig the bones out of the rock, coat them with tar or some other crude preservative, and stick them together on a steel framework for people to view. Nowadays, scientists study all parts of the skeleton and surrounding rock. Sometimes they can determine what the animal looked like when it was alive and how it lived.

A local hospital offered to perform a CT scan – a special kind of x-ray technique – to let us look inside the fossils. We hope to see the shape of the inside of Marilyn's skull and braincase thanks to the scan. It will give us a better idea of the size and shape of her brain and might even provide clues about which of her senses were well developed. Other tests indicate that Marilyn was an elderly dinosaur – some of her bones were scarred from disease. We also think SHE was a HE!

### SCIENCE TODAY

#### NO DINOSAUR STOMPING GROUND

Scientists are rushing here to study our new tyrannosaur, nicknamed "Marilyn." "We want to learn all we can about Marilyn," says Professor Dino Rockwell. "It would be ideal if we could find some of her footprints." Unfortunately, the river sediments where we discovered her bones are not the kind of rocks in which fossilized footprints are usually found. The only tyrannosaur footprint discovered in the United States is a single print in a 9-ft. (3-m) block of stone, found in New Mexico in 1983. Its length indicates that particular dinosaur's minimum stride. Scientists used the known stride length to estimate the animal's height and weight and to calculate that it probably walked at a speed of about 7 mph (11 kph).

adult human footprint

T. rex footprint

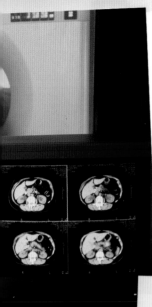

## CT SCANS

**C**omputed Axial Tomography scanners use x rays to create a number of 2D (two-dimensional) cross-section (like bread slices) images of the insides of bodies or other objects. A special computer rearranges and stacks the slices, or profiles, to create virtual 3-D pictures, which can be viewed from any angle. CT scans give doctors and scientists a good idea of the shape of internal structures.

Microscopic analyses of the matrix revealed pollen grains from plants found in Marilyn's landscape. She lived in mixed deciduous and coniferous woodlands with an undergrowth of plants like buttercups.

Before X rays and CT scans were invented, scientists smashed fossils to look inside!

Coprolites are fossilized droppings. They tell us what dinosaurs ate.

### Investigations by Dr. Marilyn Petronella

We found coprolites containing hadrosaur bone near Marilyn. If these were her droppings, it means she fed on the duck-billed dinosaurs, such as the <u>Hadrosaurus</u>.

<u>Hadrosaurus</u>

A distortion at the distal (away from the body) end of Marilyn's tibia indicates that she was quite old and may have suffered from gout.

Scientists argue about whether or not the size of this chevron indicates that it is a male or a female dinosaur. If this means ours is a male, we should name it after Charlie!

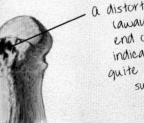

Tailbones

Some label this chevron the penis retractor bone.

# LIFE AND DEATH

## The whole story

By looking at the fossilized bones, the sediments, and the plant specimens buried nearby, we can put Marilyn's life story together. HE lived on a river plain, and – lucky for us – the river sediment buried him soon after he died.

Normally when an animal dies, scavenging animals eat most of the corpse. What is left rots away. Only animals that are buried quickly after death become fossilized – making complete dinosaur skeletons very rare.

Our display boards show the steps involved in taphonomy (the stages of decay leading up to fossilization) and diagenesis (the process by which soft sediments solidify into rocks and by which minerals replace bone) that turned our dinosaur into a fossil.

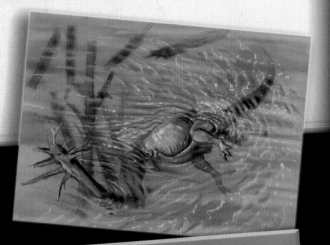

**1.** The tyrannosaur dies, probably of old age or disease, and falls into a flooded river. A tangle of jammed logs snares the floating body.

**2.** As the flooding subsides, the Sun beats down on the body partly buried in river sediment. The Sun's heat also dries the backbone tendons, which shrink and pull the neck and tail into a curve.

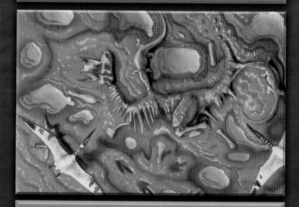

**3.** Scavengers like crocodiles, flying pterosaurs, and meat-eating dinosaurs such as *Troodon* eat any meat left on the exposed part of the carcass. Some bones are broken or carried away by animals or water.

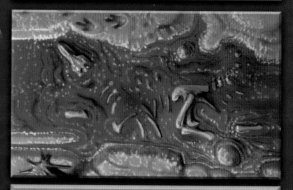

**4.** More flooding brings additional sediment that completely covers the remains. Shifting sands disarticulate and scatter the bones. Animals walking on the surface affect placement of buried bones.

## 50 MILLION YEARS AGO

**5.** Sediments eventually cover the entire site. The area's geography changes as the land sinks beneath the sea. Marine sediments build up. Sediments and bones begin to compress.

## 30 MILLION YEARS AGO

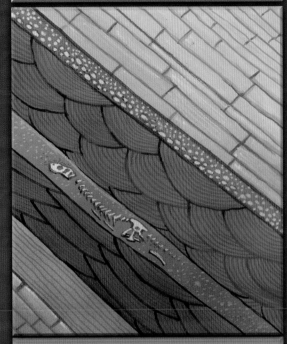

**6.** Enormous pressure crushes and cements the sediments into rock. Minerals replace the organic matter in the bones. Earthquakes force the rock layers upward into a mountain range.

## 2 MILLION YEARS AGO

**7.** Weather begins to wear away the rock of the mountain range. Frost splits the stone apart. Rivers wash away the rubble that tumbles down. The fossil skeleton comes closer and closer to the surface.

## ONE HUNDRED YEARS AGO

**8.** For the first time in 75 million years, the skeleton is exposed. We were lucky to discover our dinosaur fossils when we did. In another few thousand years, it would have eroded to dust.

# A NEW TYRANNOSAURID

## A big night

It's time to tell the world about our tyrannosaur. Dr. Petronella and Dino plan to present their scientific paper on this discovery at the annual meeting of the International Association of Vertebrate Paleontology (IAVP). They will also publish their paper in the IAVP journal (an educational magazine for scientists).

The paper is written in scientific jargon so that scientists from around the world who read it will know exactly what is being described. Dr. Petronella and Dino have also issued a press release — a much simpler version of their discovery — so that newspapers and television stations can report the story of our dinosaur.

The proper dinosaur name for our tyrannosaur is <u>Phobosaurus charlii</u>: from <u>phobos</u> (meaning fearful in Greek), <u>sauros</u> (meaning lizard in Greek), and charlii — after me!

## OH REX! WHAT BIG TEETH YOU HAVE!

**A** new arrival to *T. rex's* family tree made a big hit at a packed session of the International Association of Vertebrate Paleontology. *Phobosaurus charlii* is named after part-time research assistant Charlie Smith, who discovered an upper jawbone among other artifacts stored in the City Museum's storeroom since the 1920s. Smith's discovery launched the recent expedition to Montana to locate the rest of the dinosaur. The well-preserved skeleton is being prepared for display. What the newcomer lacks in size it makes up for in bite: *P. charlii's* teeth are bigger and more numerous than those of our favorite meat eater, *T. rex.*

### *PHOBOSAURUS CHARLII*

Smith holds the prepared skull of *Phobosaurus charlii*. Paleontologists from around the world examined this recent fossil discovery.

# TITLE: A NEW TYRANNOSAURID FROM THE UPPER CAMPANIAN AGE OF THE LATE CRETACEOUS PERIOD IN MONTANA

**AUTHORS**
**ADDRESSES**

M.P. PETRONELLA[1] and D. ROCKWELL[2]
1. The City Museum
2. The Dinosaur Museum of Montana

**ABSTRACT** - A new Upper Campanian tyrannosaurid, *Phobosaurus charlii*, gen. et sp. nov., is described on the basis of a forty-percent-complete skeleton excavated in northeastern Montana. While the postcranial skeleton presents a conservative tyrannosaurid anatomy, the maxilla is characterized by relatively large teeth. Cladistic analyses place *P. charlii* between *Albertosaurus* and *Daspletosaurus*.

## INTRODUCTION

The serendipitous discovery of a tyrannosaur maxilla in City Museum led to the reappraisal of material gathered during a 1920s expedition to Montana. This material remained largely unpublished and the unofficial identification seemed somewhat spurious. Investigators used original expedition photographs and field notes which led to the discovery of a scree slope below an eroding cliff of fluvial and lacustrine shales, sandstones, and the Upper Campanian, similar to those of search of the country rock in situ.

## SKELETAL RECONSTRUCTION

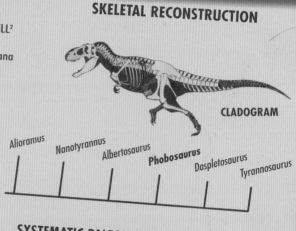

**CLADOGRAM**

Alioramus  Nanotyrannus  Albertosaurus  **Phobosaurus**  Daspletosaurus  Tyrannosaurus

## SYSTEMATIC PALEONTOLOGY

*Saurischia seelii*, 1888
*Theropoda marshii*, 1881
*Tyrannosauridae osbornii*, 1906
*Phobosaurus charlii*, gen. et sp. nov.

**Etymology:** from *phobos* (Greek, meaning fearful), *sauros* (Gr., meaning lizard) and *charlii* (after Charlie, the research assistant who maxilla in the storeroom of the City Museum's store- preserved left maxilla.

## Opening day

It seems like such a long time ago that I found that upper jawbone (oops — maxilla) in the City Museum's storeroom. So much has happened since then — the trips to Montana, the hot-air balloon rides, the search for the fossils, the excavation and shipping of our discovery — but at last our assembled dinosaur is on display. Or is it?

Our display skeleton is actually a plastic reproduction of the original set of fossils. Charlie's real bones are very valuable and are set aside for paleontological study by researchers from around the world.

Two complete skeletons have been constructed from our discovery. One is prominently displayed in Dino's museum in Montana, and the other is here in our own City Museum. MEET CHARLIE!

Reconstruction of <u>Phobosaurus charlii</u>.

Fiberglass and plastic reconstructions of actual bones are shown in white.

Technicians studied the known fossil in order to accurately build the missing parts.

Red bones mark those missing from our specimen. Tyrannosaur bones found in other museums served as models for our casts.

10 ft (3 m)

26 ft (8 m)

**From: Charlie Smith**
**Subject: Conflicting information?**

Dear Dr. Petronella — I just received a request from a student paleontologist for information regarding our classification of the tyrannosaurids, specifically our *Phobosaurus maxilla* (CM-008M). He suspects that *Charlii* is not a new *Phobosaurus* at all but an undiscovered branch of the *Daspletosaurus* genus. An e-mail from another researcher says that what we identified as the penis retractor bone is instead a bone that helped females lay eggs. So Charlie is a female after all?!? What do we do now? Have we got it all wrong?

**From: Dr. Marilyn Petronella**
**Subject: Welcome to the world of science**

Dear Charlie — Please don't worry. Scientists disagree all the time. We learn by questioning new scientific evidence and testing new theories against old ones. The exciting thing is that we will never know everything. THERE WILL ALWAYS BE NEW DISCOVERIES AND CHALLENGES — IT'S HOW SCIENCE WORKS!

USER 1

USER 2

USER 3

# GLOSSARY

**amber:** fossilized plant resin.

**anatomical:** indicating an exact body section, organ, or division.

**articulated:** joined together to give an example of a shape or form.

**badlands:** an area of uneven landscape formed by wind and water erosion.

**bed (fossil):** the layer of (usually) sedimentary rock in which a fossil is buried.

**braincase:** the skull or bones surrounding the brain.

**Campanian Age:** a subdivision of the late Cretaceous period, when dinosaurs lived, from 83.5 to 71.3 million years ago.

**carnivore:** a meat-eating animal.

**carrion:** decaying animal flesh.

**caudal:** relating to the tail area.

**cervical:** relating to the neck area.

**coniferous:** a tree or shrub that produces cones. It usually remains green year-round.

**crest:** a ridge along the top of a skull.

**Cretaceous Period:** the last of the three major divisions of geological time, from 145 to 65 million years ago, in which dinosaurs lived.

**deposition:** the process by which moving water lays down layers of sand, mud, and silt.

**diagenesis:** the process through which sediment becomes rock, and bones become fossils.

**disarticulated:** not joined together; scattered.

**environment:** all the conditions — climate, food supply, landscape, other animals and plants — in which an animal or a plant lives.

**erosion:** the wearing away of a rock or landscape by weather, water, plants, or animal movement.

**excavation:** the removal of the top layers to expose what's underneath.

**fossil:** the remains of an animal, plant, or footprints preserved in rock.

**fossilized:** to become a fossil.

**geologist:** someone who studies rocks and the structure of Earth.

**Global Positioning System (GPS):** an electronic navigational tool that pinpoints any position on Earth by using satellite signals.

**gout:** a disorder that causes the buildup of uric acid crystals in the joints, causing pain.

**gully:** a ditch formed by running water.

**herbivore:** a plant-eating animal.

**jargon:** the specialized language, names, and abbreviations used by specific groups, such as technicians, scientists, or medical personnel.

**matrix:** the material — usually rock — in which a fossil is embedded.

**meander:** a twisting, turning, and winding path.

**mineral:** a natural substance found in the ground that is neither plant nor animal.

**overburden:** layers of rock and soil above the bed containing fossils.

**oxidize:** to cause a chemical change by combining with oxygen.

**paleoichnologist:** someone who studies and researches fossilized footprints.

**paleontologist:** someone who studies animal and plant life of the past.

**paleontology:** the study of fossils and ancient life.

**pinnacle:** the highest point of a land formation.

**pollen:** flower particles that fertilize other flowers. Fossilized pollen grains found by paleontologists give clues to ancient plant life.

**preserve:** to protect from breakdown, decay, or decomposition.

**pygmy:** a small-sized form of a plant or animal.

**rappel:** to descend a cliff using a system of ropes.

**ravine:** a very steep, narrow valley.

**reconstruction:** in paleontology, to recreate an animal or plant using fossils as models.

**sandstone:** a sedimentary rock made from solidified sand.

**scale:** to climb something little by little.

**scree:** loose stones or rocky debris found at the foot of a slope or cliff.

**sediment:** particles of sand or mud that accumulate at the bottom of a river, lake, or ocean that can compress and harden to form sedimentary rock.

**sedimentary:** layers formed by deposits of sand, rock, silt, and other particles that solidify.

**silt:** a type of sediment with particles that are finer than sand but coarser than mud.

**specimen:** a sample of something used for scientific study.

**superposition:** on top of, or above; in sedimentary rock, the youngest layer gets deposited superior to the older layers.

**taphonomy:** the different stages — such as burial, decay, and disarticulation — of the breakdown of an animal or plant before the fossilization process begins.

**theropod:** a dinosaur with small front limbs that walked on its hind legs.

**tyrannosaurid:** any of the members of a family of dinosaurs known as tyrannosaurs, or terrible lizards.

**tyrant:** a very brutal ruler.

**vertebrae:** the many bones that form the back, or spine, of an animal and through which runs the spinal cord.

The following words and terms help explain the scientific document on page 27:

**abstract:** a summary of an article's contents.

**cladogram:** a diagram — based on shared characteristics — that shows how the animal is related to others.

**etymology:** the origin, root words, and meaning of a word or a name.

**holotype:** a specimen that represents the general characteristics of a group.

**skeletal reconstruction:** to reassemble the bones of an animal.

**systematic paleontology:** a way to classify a plant or animal by grouping together similar traits.

# MORE INFORMATION

## BOOKS

*Buried Blueprints: Maps and Sketches of Lost Worlds and Mysterious Places.* Albert Lorenz. (Abrams)

*The Complete Idiot's Guide to Dinosaurs. Complete Idiot's Guides* (series). Jay Stevenson (MacMilan)

*Dinosaur Encyclopedia.* David Lambert (DK Publishing)

*Dinosaurs.* (series). Dougal Dixon. (Gareth Stevens)

*Exploring Dinosaur National Monument. Exploring* (series). Bert Gildart (Falcon)

*National Geographic Dinosaurs.* Paul M. Barrett (National Geographic)

*The Science of Jurassic Park: And the Lost World, Or, How to Build a Dinosaur.* Rob Desalle (Basic Books)

*World of Dinosaurs.* (series). (Gareth Stevens)

## WEB SITES

www.enchantedlearning.com/subjects/dinosaurs/ anatomy/Locomotion.shtml
Calculate the speed of a dinosaur and learn how it moved.

sunsite.berkeley.edu/KidsClick!/
Type "dinosaurs" into the search box for more web sites.

www.yahooligans.com/content/science/dinosaurs/index.html
Dinopedia offers a variety of information, including a glossary and links to the different geologic time periods.

www.brainpop.com/science/plantsandanimals/dinosaurs
View a quick flick about these "terrible lizards."

## VIDEOS

*Walking With Dinosaurs.* (Warner)

*When Dinosaurs Roamed America.* (Artisan Entertainment)

# INDEX